the skinny on

KEY TERMS

Amortization: the paying down of a loan amount.

Appraisal: analysis of the market value of a property.

ARM: Adjustable Rate Mortgage – the interest rate is fixed for some period (usually one to five years) and then adjusts annually.

Mortgagee: the person who owns the mortgage, i.e. the lender.

Mortgagor: the party who puts a mortgage on a house, i.e. the borrower.

Mortgage Security: an investment the returns on which are tied to bundles of mortgages on homes.

Mortgage Interest Deduction: a government incentive to home-ownership that gives owners an annual tax deduction for interest payments (so long as mortgage not in excess of $1,000,000).

Negative Amortization: when the loan amount increases instead of decreases.

NINJA loans: acronym for how crazy some lenders got when they made loans to borrowers who had "no income, no job, no assets."

www.theskinnyon.com

Pssst ... get the skinny on life's most important lessons

www.theskinnyon.com

The Easiest Learning There Is!!

"Don't let the stick figures fool you ... Jim Randel will have you laughing and thinking at the same time. A very enjoyable read!"

Ken Blanchard, author
The One Minute Manager®

"I've tracked Jimmy's incredible run of successful real estate investments for twenty years."

Jeff Dunne, Vice Chairman, CB Richard Ellis

Payment Option Loan: gives the borrower flexibility as to how much to pay the lender.

PMI (Private Mortgage Insurance): payments due from a borrower required by some lenders when the loan-to-value of a first mortgage exceeds a specific threshold (usually 80%).

Prepayment Penalty: a fee in some mortgage loans that must be paid to the lender if a loan is paid off sooner than a stipulated period (usually one to three years).

Ratings Agency: supposedly impartial arbiter of the risk grading of certain investment products including mortgage securities.

Stated Income Loans: loans for which the borrower does not have to produce written verification of the income he claims to be earning.

Tranche: one portion of a mortgage security – all the loans in a specific tranche are of similar risk metrics (e.g. down payment amount, credit score of borrower, etc.).

The Skinny on the Housing Crisis

the skinny on™

the housing crisis

what every homeowner and homebuyer needs to know

Jim Randel

ENDORSEMENTS

"Jim Randel has created a brilliant and super simple book called The Skinny on the Housing Crisis … this book is a must own to everyone who is looking to buy a house or anyone who has a home currently."

Virginia Mortgage & Loans Blog

"Jim Randel takes the complex issues related to the housing crisis and presents them in an easy-to-understand manner. The book is well written, it can be read in under one hour, and the reader is left with a basic understanding of the mess we are in today … I highly recommend *The Skinny on the Housing Crisis*."

Laurence Roberts, author The Great Housing Bubble

"I had the pleasure of reading one of the most enjoyable, easy to read, and informative books the other day. Similar to the "for Dummies" line of books, but much more engaging, (*The Skinny on the Housing Crisis*) is an absolute hoot. … This book taught ME a few things, and I thought I was pretty savvy about real estate."

Myrtle Beach Real Estate Blog

"*The Skinny on the Housing Crisis* … popular presentation of some very complex stuff."

Andrew Waite, Publisher, Real Estate Investor Magazine

"Anyone who has a hard time wading through the dense Fed-speak and high-finance talk now saturating the airwaves, the Internet and the nation's newspapers, but still wants to know what happened to the housing industry, can find answers in Jim Randel's latest book, *The Skinny on the Housing Crisis*."

Pam Dawkins, The Connecticut Post

"The Skinny books are fast, fun and informative."

Jerry Zezima, Syndicated Columnist

"*The Skinny on the Housing Crisis*… Recommended for anyone considering the purchase, sale or financing of real estate."

Free Money Finance Blog

ISBN: 978-0-9818935-2-5
Illustration: Jeannette Zolan

For information address RAND Publishing, 265 Post Road West, Westport, CT, 06880 or call (203) 226-8727.

The Skinny On™ books are available for special promotions and premiums. For details contact: Donna Hardy, call (203) 222-6295 or visit our website: www.theskinnyon.com

Printed in the United States of America

the skinny on™

Welcome to a new series of publications entitled **The Skinny On™,** a progression of drawings, dialogue and text intended to convey information in a concise fashion.

In our time-starved and information-overloaded culture, most of us have far too little time to read and absorb major important writings and research on important topics. So, our understanding tends to float on the surface – without the benefit of the thinking of the writers and teachers who have spent years studying these topics.

Our series is intended to address this situation. Our team of readers and researchers has done a ton of homework in preparing our books for you. We have read just about everything respected author on a particular topic and distilled what we learned into this "skinny" book for your benefit.

You might think of our book as concentrated learning. By spending one or two hours reading our book, we maintain that you get the benefit of the hundreds of hours you would spend reading all the works on a particular subject.

Our goal is to do the reading for you, cull out what is important, distill the key points and present them in a book that we hope is both instructive and entertaining.

Although minimalist in design, we do take our message very seriously. Please do not confuse format with content. The time you invest reading this book will be paid back to you many, many times over.

FOREWORD

Spring, 2009: Wow, how things have changed! The housing boom has bust "big time" and the median price of an existing U.S. house is (on average) down from a high of about $225,000 to about $175,000. The decrease is even greater in areas that experienced substantial appreciation.

The new Administration is trying to slow down foreclosures with incentives to lenders and holders of mortgage securities (we'll learn more about these in the pages to follow) to restructure loans. Time will tell if this approach works. A year or two from now we will look back at what happened and catch our breath.

What is most important is that we learn from our mistakes. How did the housing boom start? Who made money and who lost money? Why did so few of our best thinkers see the bust coming? What can we do to prevent busts in the future? How can each of us improve our own knowledge as real estate buyers and sellers so that we maximize opportunities and avoid danger areas?

Because the housing world is changing so quickly, we worry that information you read today could become out of date in a couple of months. For that reason, you may wish to register at our website for free updates (every 90 days) on trends, new laws and current events. The point is to keep you on top of all that is going on so that your transactions in the housing world can be as profitable as possible.

INTRODUCTION

As this book goes to publication in the spring of 2009, the United States is struggling with the hangover from one heck of a party: a long housing boom starting in 2000. From 2000 to 2006 home prices grew almost 15% per year and about 3,000,000 households became new homeowners. What could be bad about that?

What could be bad is that the foundation for these increases was shaky. Housing prices were fueled in large part by easy credit mixed with buyer mania and speculation. During that same period, mortgage debt rose from $6 trillion in 2000 to $13 trillion in 2006 – premised on the belief that housing values would always go up.

The problem with every boom, however, is the inevitable bust that follows.

Beginning in 2006 U.S. housing prices began to fall. According to the Case-Shiller Housing Index, the median price of housing in the United States has dropped (on average) about 30% from the 2nd Quarter of 2006 to the 2nd Quarter of 2009. As a result, about 1 in 4 homes with a mortgage are worth less than the amount of debt on the property.

The above statistics are the big picture which is, of course, the aggregate of tens of thousands of individual stories of normal people. We are going to decipher the big picture by looking at the story of one such couple, Billy and Beth, normal in most respects – they just happen to be stick people.

Finally, I want to make it clear that in the story which follows, the illustrated personalities are meant to be caricatures. I am very well aware that there are great, hard-working and very honest people in all the professions and businesses represented in our story. But, as with all parodies, there is some amount of truth that we must all accept.

JANUARY, 2006

"OUR STORY BEGINS..."

"That's me,
Jim Randel." →

THIS IS BILLY AND BETH. THEY ARE NEWLY MARRIED. BILLY JUST GOT A NEW JOB AND THEY HAVE HIGH HOPES FOR THE FUTURE. THEY HAVE HEARD THAT REAL ESTATE IS A GOOD INVESTMENT.

2

AND SO THEY ARE TRYING TO EDUCATE THEMSELVES.

3

THEY EVEN STAY UP LATE TO WATCH THE REAL ESTATE EXPERTS ON TV.

4

"Wow, real estate sure is a great investment!"

5

Well, Billy, yes you can. Almost all channels sell time for infomercials without liability for content. What's more, the Federal agency overseeing broadcast content, the FCC, does not have the resources to police all of these offerings.

As described in Newsweek correspondent Daniel McGinn's book, *House Lust* (Doubleday, 2008) there have been many real estate gurus on TV over the years: "Over time many…fell on hard times. Some went bankrupt or faced tax evasion charges; at least one went to prison."

12

But, whenever one guru falls by the wayside,

another always springs up.

13

"Just 2 years ago I was living in my car. Then I discovered a foolproof strategy for buying real estate."

14

"WOW!"

"Today I own 10 cars…. and 3 houses!"

15

THE NEXT DAY BILLY AND BETH GO FOR A WALK.

FOR SALE

16

"Let's call the phone # on the sign and find out what the price is."

"OK."

FOR SALE

17

18

19

20

21

Can Charlotte say what she did? Well, yes she can. Note that she was careful to use the word "probably" and in that situation, courts will most likely rule her comment to be just an opinion.

In fact, just recently a court in Vista, California dismissed the case of a homebuyer who claimed that her agent misled her on values ... the court ruled that the agent was just giving his best guess.

22

23

Charlotte has little to do during the next two days but she recently attended a Realtor's® Convention where a sales trainer suggested that a problem with agents is they are too available, proposing that the key to success is an appointment.

"Do attorneys and doctors see you on your schedule or theirs?" he asks. "Theirs, of course."

Charlotte figures that if Billy and Beth have to wait to meet with her, they will be more likely to appreciate her expertise.

Charlotte is an expert tennis player.

"We'll be there!"

Some might suggest that using a real estate company's in-house mortgage "advisor" is not a great idea.

Since almost all of these in-house advisors work as mortgage brokers, that is on a commission basis, they are beholden to the real estate agents who direct business their way and therefore may be reluctant to give borrowers objective advice.

TEN MINUTES LATER

"Welcome to Best Homes Mortgage Assistance. I'm Ralph."

"Hi Ralph, We're not sure we're ready to buy. Billy just got a new job, and I'm hoping to quit my job and apply to law school."

36

Just what we don't need in this country… another lawyer… UGH!!

37

"Law school.... Great.
Congratulations."

38

"Beth is nervous about
my new job, Ralph."

39

It's obvious that she's the brighter of the two, but if I suggest they wait a few months to buy, their agent, Charlotte, will poke my eyes out.

40

"No worries. We have mortgage products tailor-made for your exact situation."

41

You judge whether Beth has a point:

The higher the interest rate the mortgage broker can "sell" to the borrower, the more money the mortgage broker makes.

For example, let's assume that for a good credit borrower, a lender is willing to make a 30-year fixed rate loan at 5.75% and to pay a mortgage brokerage fee of .5% of the loan amount. Think of the 5.75% as a "wholesale" rate.

The lender sends out to mortgage brokers a rate sheet which indicates the fee the mortgage broker will receive for bringing borrowers to the lender, at varying interest rates. A rate sheet might appear as follows:

Rate	Mortgage Broker's Fee (% of loan amt.)
5.75%	0.50
6.00%	0.75
6.25%	1.00
7.25%	2.00

Note that the greater the spread between the wholesale rate and the rate the borrower agrees to pay (think retail rate), the greater the fee to the mortgage broker.

If a borrower has marginal credit or is unsophisticated, a mortgage broker can push the spread between the wholesale and retail rates. In the example above, a mortgage broker might convince a vulnerable borrower that the "going rate" was 7.25% and make a fee equal to 2% of the loan amount.

A mortgage broker should disclose its fee to the borrower. This fee should also be identified in advance of closing on a form titled "Good Faith Estimate."

A 1% fee is reasonable.

"My point is this:

When working with a mortgage broker ASK about his rate sheet, what your choices are, and how he gets paid for the various loan products he is discussing with you."

Can a borrower get a lower interest rate by going straight to a lender? Not from lenders who work with mortgage brokers. These lenders know that in order to attract business from mortgage brokers, they cannot undercut the rates brokers pass on to consumers.

But recently (spring of 2009), some lenders have stopped working with mortgage brokers. These lenders claim that loans originated by brokers have a higher default rate than those they originate themselves.

If you are shopping for a loan today, you should check with both mortgage brokers and with banks in order to get a good read on market rates.

BILLY AND BETH AT HOME THAT EVENING

"Billy I feel like we may be getting in over our heads."

"Don't worry, Beth, Ralph is a professional. I'm sure he knows what he's doing."

Is Ralph a professional?

Whereas there are ethical and knowledgeable mortgage brokers, there are also creeps. The problem is that the mortgage brokerage business is largely unregulated. With very low barriers to entry and little training, people across the entire ethical spectrum became mortgage brokers during the housing boom.

According to one estimate the number of mortgage brokers working in the United States tripled in the five-year period from 2001-2006.

49

Richard Bitner, a former mortgage lender, has written a book which explains much about the 2001-2006 housing boom, *Confessions of a Subprime Lender* (Wiley, 2008). Bitner knew that the mortgage brokerage business was heading in the wrong direction when he saw a sign near his home in Dallas:

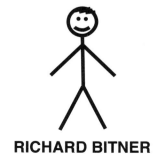

RICHARD BITNER

WELCOME
TO U.S. CENTER

*HAIR
*NAILS
*MORTGAGES

50

But, Billy and Beth, like many first-time buyers, are trusting.

Charlotte and Ralph seem like such nice people.

"Beth, I have a good feeling about working with Ralph. A guy in my office told me that his cousin, Sal, went to a mortgage broker who helped him buy a brand new house with no money down."

Let's learn more about Sal.

"Hi. I'm Arnold, the A in ABC Mortgage."

"Hi, I'm Sal"

55

"What do you do for a living, Sal?"

"I'm an investment banker."

56

57

58

"No problem. That's why we have STATED INCOME LOANS."

"STATED INCOME LOANS" were originally conceived as a product to address loan requests from self-employed individuals whose income might legitimately vary from year to year. Over time others availed themselves of this loan product and it became known in the industry as a "liar's loan."

Sal is not really an investment banker. He does not make $300,000. He owns a chicken farm and makes $40,000 in a good year.

But he feels that he is ready to move on in life and he has been reading *The Secret* (Atria, 2006) and visualizing big things for himself.

As the housing boom attracted more and more buyers – some of whom had very marginal credit, the lending world invented loan products to cover all situations.

Eventually some marketing genius created the ultimate: a NINJA loan.

No Income, No Job, No Assets

By now you may be wondering why lenders would make loans that might never be repaid?

Excellent Question!

Why mortgage lenders would make loans that seemed likely to run into trouble:

1. Whereas once lenders would hold loans and collect the payments, that business model changed in the last few decades. By the time of the 2000-2006 housing boom, many lenders were just conduits: originating loans then packaging and selling them to investors.

2. Under this originate-and-sell scenario, once the sale was made, the lender would usually not have an ongoing interest in whether the borrower paid his mortgage ... or not.

Should the mortgage broker, Arnold, have checked Sal's statements of employment and income?

Well, yes. And if he was in the business for the long term, he would have. Unfortunately, Arnold was not. His talent was sales and he figured that when the housing market cooled, he would go back to working in his brother's shoe store. As with lenders who sold loans, mortgage brokers usually had no continuing interest in whether the loan was paid... or not.

SAL'S CLOSING

"Congratulations, Sal. You just bought a $1,000,000 home with a $900,000 first mortgage and a $100,000 piggyback mortgage."

ARNOLD

What is a "piggyback" mortgage?

A "piggyback" mortgage is a second mortgage.

What is a second mortgage?

65

A second mortgage "sits behind" a first mortgage.

The important point to understand is that in the event a property has to be sold to satisfy the debts against it (think foreclosure), the first mortgage must be paid in full (including all principal owed, interest, fees and collection costs) before the second mortgage gets anything.

66

The key to determining who gets paid first –
i.e., which is the first and which is the second
mortgage – is the timing of filing of the mortgage documents. Whichever document is
filed first in the Clerk's Office where the property
is located has first priority on funds.

There can also be 3d and 4th mortgages and
so on. The key in all situations is that the
sequence of filing determines who gets
proceeds from the sale of a property. Once
the first mortgagee (lender) gets paid, if any
is left over, then the next lender gets paid,
and so on.

Now as we saw, Arnold was able to get Sal
$1,000,000 in debt to purchase a $1,000,000
house. Given Sal's $300,000 in annual "income,"
Arnold was able to convince a lender to give
Sal a 90% first mortgage and a 10% second
mortgage - or piggyback loan.

These piggyback second mortgages were
often made in lieu of a larger first mortgage
as a way to avoid private mortgage insurance
(required when the loan-to-value of a single
mortgage exceeds a threshold). There is no
logic to this approach.

FAST FORWARD 6 MONTHS

Although Sal read *The Secret* three times and asked the "Universe" to send him money, his requests were not answered.

Soon Sal fell behind in his mortgage payments.

When a borrower gets behind in his payments, he is "in arrears." Eventually Sal's lender initiated a foreclosure action, obtained title to the house and had Sal evicted.

Foreclosure: "The legal process by which a mortgage lender obtains ownership of a house from a borrower who is in arrears."

Current estimates suggest that if housing prices continue to fall, as many as five million home-owners could lose their homes to foreclosure.

Sal's home buying experience turned him bitter.

He feels he was abused by "the man."

Sal's feeling that the system mistreated him is obviously unfounded.

His statements of employment and income were not just honest mistakes. Sal committed fraud: an intentional misrepresentation or deceit.

Is the story of the 2000 – 2009 housing boom and bust one of widespread fraud and criminal activity by individuals like Sal?

I don't think so. Certainly there was some amount of criminality but it was a small part of the whole story – and when it happened it was usually the work of teams organized to deceive.

The scam usually went like this:

Seller selling house for $400,000. Scam Buyer goes to Seller and says:

"Let's enter a contract for $500,000. I have an appraiser buddy who will support that number. I will then apply for a 95% loan ($475,000). After we close the loan, I will give you $425,000 and I will keep the extra $50,000."

Seller: "But isn't that dishonest?"

Scam Buyer: "Do you want $425,000 or don't you?"

And some sellers went along. Sometimes the mortgage broker and real estate agent were also part of the Scam Buyer's team.

By the time the mortgage lender realized it had a problem, the Scam Buyer and Seller were gone from view. And upon foreclosure, the lender (who had loaned $475,000) owned a house worth at best $400,000 and probably much less.

Unfortunately, there will always be scammers.

Back to Billy and Beth

"Billy, maybe we should rent for another year. Until you are more established at your new job."

75

"Gee, Beth…. everything in the news is about prices going higher. If we wait, it could be too late."

76

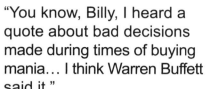

"You know, Billy, I heard a quote about bad decisions made during times of buying mania… I think Warren Buffett said it."

77

The guy who sings Margaritaville????

78

"And, he's considered one of the world's smartest investors."

79

"But, Beth, it says right here in USA Today that housing is one of the best investments a person can make. I don't think renting makes any sense at all."

80

Billy is certainly right about the media getting behind housing during the boom years. For many years all the business journalists wrote that buying one's own home was a great personal investment.

Until, that is, the media decided that the new "hot" story was the length of the housing boom. Then the headlines wondered out loud:

"When Will the Housing Boom Bust?"

As we will see, some blame this shift in media emphasis for the start of the bust.

"But Billy, a house is not income producing. Some writers suggest that young people use their savings to create income opportunities."

"Wait a minute. You're not reading that *Rich Dad, Poor Dad* book are you?"

83

"Well, yes I am. And the author, Robert Kiyosaki, says that a house should be considered a liablility since it's not income-producing."

84

There is merit to both Billy and Beth's points of view. When real estate is appreciating, home ownership makes good sense.

Instead of paying rent to a third party, by paying yourself "rent," you pay down a mortgage and ride the tide of rising values.

And up until about 2007 most anyone who bought a house in the preceding five or six years was very happy about that decision.

But, there are also times when renting makes sense. For example, if you are unsure about how long you will be in one location, renting enhances your mobility.

And, Robert Kiyosaki makes an important point too: when one has limited capital (e.g., a young person), sometimes it is best spent in the purchase or development of income-producing assets.

"But, Beth, my Uncle Morty is an accountant and he says that even our Federal laws favor homeowners."

Billy's Uncle Morty is correct: our federal income-tax laws do favor homeownership with deductions (offsets against income) for mortgage interest and real estate taxes. Some argue that this policy is unfair to renters.

Someone who is paying rent is funding his landlord's mortgage and real estate taxes but, as a tenant, will receive no deductions.

The deductibility of mortgage interest and real estate taxes is one way that the government encourages home-ownership.

What is Zillow.com?

Zillow.com is a website started three years ago by two ex-Microsoft executives.

It has become very popular in a short period of time. It claims to have sales data on 80,000,000 houses and to be able to estimate values of houses based on sales of comparable properties.

The Zillow.com valuation is called a "Zestimate."

CHARLOTTE IS READY FOR BETH'S "ZILLOW TALK."

"Well, Beth, there are some problems with the Zillow estimates."

99

100

Can Billy and Beth trust Charlotte... or, is she just trying to make a sale?

Well, of course, that depends upon the agent.

In researching his book about the home-buying process, *House Lust*, Daniel McGinn attended the annual convention of the National Association of Realtors® and concluded:

"It's a meeting of (Realtors) whose members belong to a species that often behave with a slightly different set of instincts from traditional Homo Sapiens."

And Stephen Dubner and Steven Levitt are not much more flattering in their best-selling book *Freakonomics* (Wiley, 2005).

"A real estate agent may see you not so much as an ally but as a mark."

IS THIS CRITICISM FAIR?

The criticism may be a little unfair. As one who has dealt with real estate agents for twenty-five years, I believe the point should be made that the business model under which agents operate sometimes produces inappropriate behavior (even so, there are many hard-working and honorable agents).

Here is how I see it:

1. There are too many real estate agents. In 2000 there were 750,000. By 2005 there were about 1,250,000. That means an extra 500,000 agents fighting over roughly the same number of transactions.

2. Real estate agents operate under an all-or-nothing compensation model. Whenever this is the case, there will be people who act unethically – pushing as hard as they can to make a deal, notwithstanding the best interests of their buyer or seller customer.

3. Real estate agents want (and perhaps deserve) the same respect as other professionals, but the States have not required the kind of training or licensing that might keep the less capable or not-quite-honorable agents out of the business.

Also, the major trade group for real estate agents, the National Association of Realtors® can be criticized for creating a mindset pushing transactions - no matter what.

For example, in the fall of 2006 (when prices were beginning to fall) the NAR was running full-page ads prodding buyers to act immediately.

> Large Inventory Won't Last!
> Prices Overall have Stabilized!

Anyone who followed the NAR's advice would most likely be unhappy right now.

Billy and Beth are now at an important crossroads in their life.

They want to own a house of course. In fact, they want their own house very badly.

Beth, however, believes that they may be overpaying for 100 Main Street. Billy believes that even if they are, it will go up in value. Charlotte has convinced him of that. What should Billy and Beth do now?

Well, they should not act impulsively and jump at the first house they visit. Beth was taking an important first step when she went to Zillow.com in an initial search for information. Here are other steps they could take:

1. Talk with **disinterested** real estate agents, escrow agents and attorneys about the state of the market in their town.

2. Consider hiring a disinterested real estate agent to do a **market valuation**. (Inexpensive).

3. Go view other houses that are similar in size and location to 100 Main Street (**comparables**) – how does 100 Main Street stack up?

4. Confirm **how long** 100 Main Street has been on the market and whether there have been price reductions.

In short, never put ALL of your trust in someone whose compensation depends upon you buying what he or she is selling. Do some of your own homework!

**But Billy and Beth
are anxious to buy,
and Charlotte seems
so genuine.**

As Charlotte predicted, the Seller countered Billy and Beth's offer.

And, a deal was struck at $485,000.

But, reasonable people can differ about what an independent building inspector is.

When Charlotte bought her own house she used "Excellent House Inspections." They were very diligent and uncovered problems that she used to obtain a price reduction from her seller.

But, Charlotte feels that "Excellent" is a little too picky for her buyer clients and so she recommends "Very Good House Inspections." They are good, too, and since Charlotte sends them a lot of business, they tend not to make big problems for her deals.

"Let's recap Billy and Beth's situation:

1. They are working with a real estate agent whose income depends upon them buying. That is OK so long as they do their homework to confirm what Charlotte is telling them."

2. They are working with a mortgage broker, Ralph, who works in Charlotte's office. Ralph is a nice guy but he depends on the agents in the office to send him business. He knows that if he kills a deal by, for example, advising Billy and Beth to wait to buy, his business will dry up.

3. They are aware that they need a home inspection but they will most likely use the company that Charlotte suggests – a company that, like Ralph, depends upon referrals from Charlotte to obtain new business. Billy and Beth are arguably on a slippery slope."

118

119

To Billy and Beth's delight, VERY GOOD HOUSE INSPECTIONS confirms that 100 Main Street is in "very good" condition.

THAT EVENING

Beth reads an article which says that house prices have started to soften.

"Billy, I'm worried that we're making a mistake. Housing prices are falling."

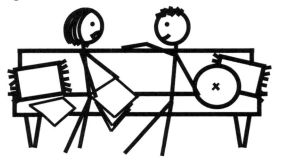

"Beth and I are having trouble sleeping. We're worried that with prices falling we are overpaying."

"Oh, you shouldn't worry. It's very common for first-time buyers to have this reaction."

124

"You're totally protected … as part of your mortgage application process an appraisal must be done, and if the house does not appraise for what you're paying, you can cancel the purchase!"

125

"Oh, thanks, Charlotte. That makes sense. I see you've thought of everything..."

"Beth, She's got us covered. The appraisal protects us."

Not so fast, Billy. An appraisal is a matter of opinion. The appraised price is less than scientific. And, some appraisers, like building inspectors, keep sight of where their bread is buttered.

During Beth and Billy's mortgage application process, Ralph – the mortgage broker at Best Homes – will be selecting an appraiser.

Will the appraiser be objective?

Here is what one author says:

"When a broker orders an appraisal, he provides an estimate or target value for the property to the appraiser. If the appraiser has problems consistently reaching his number, the broker will hire someone else. Any appraiser who goes strictly by the book can struggle to get repeat business.

"As impartial evaluators, appraisers are supposed to remain objective ... their opinion should not be influenced by anything other than the available data in the market place. This is a case where theory and reality are seldom in sync."

Confessions of a Subprime Lender (Wiley, 2008)

RICHARD BITNER

As with the real estate agent referral to the mortgage broker and to the home inspector, the concern is that the appraiser who has too close a relationship with a mortgage broker or lender may not be objective.

Last year, New York Attorney General Andrew Cuomo reached an agreement with Fannie Mae and Freddie Mac (big purchasers of mortgages) whereby they agreed not to purchase mortgages on homes unless the house had been valued by an independent appraiser – not affiliated with a mortgage broker or lender.

Billy and Beth were very happy to hear that the appraiser hired by Ralph valued 100 Main Street at $485,000.

Just before we follow Billy and Beth into the mortgage process, let's take a look at a player who was a huge part of the housing boom and bust: THE FLIPPER.

As the prices of housing began to rise quickly early this decade, it was inevitable that speculators would enter the game.

Wikipedia defines "flipping" as the practice of "buying an asset and quickly reselling it for a profit." Wikipedia also suggests that "many experts blame the U.S. real estate bubble on investor speculation and irrational flipping."

The real estate speculator or flipper either tied up a property and then tried to flip his contract or, actually closed and immediately attempted to resell. This game only works, of course, if prices rise quickly.

When prices flatten, flippers run for the exits – some losing contract deposits, some defaulting on mortgages – **in all cases increasing the level of chaos in the housing world.**

BILLY AND BETH ENTER THE MORTGAGE PROCESS

BILLY AND BETH MEET AGAIN WITH BEST HOMES MORTGAGE "ADVISOR," RALPH.

"Congratulations. Charlotte tells me that you've got 100 Main Street under contract."

133

"Yes, but we have a mortgage contingency in the contract, and we need 98% financing."

134

What is a mortgage contingency?

It is a clause in a Real Estate Contract (sometimes called Purchase & Sale Agreement) which says:

"If the BUYER does not obtain a mortgage for $X (a stipulated amount) at an interest rate of Y% with an amortization period of not less than Z years, the BUYER may terminate the herein Contract."

In other words, if this clause is in a contract, then a buyer who does not get the mortgage he needs can cancel the purchase and get his down payment back.

"Well, I've reviewed the financial information you dropped off and I have high hopes that we can get you the loan you need."

137

138

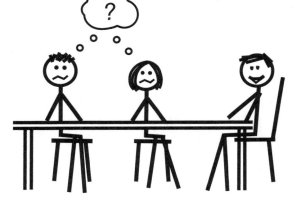

139

140

141

142

Ralph is telling the truth about Alan Greenspan.

Here is what Greenspan (Chairman of the Federal Reserve until February, 2006) had to say about adjustable rate mortgages in a speech he gave in February, 2004 titled "Understanding Household Debt Obligations:"

"One way homeowners attempt to manage their payment risk is to use fixed-rate mortgages, which typically allow homeowners to prepay their debt when interest rates fall but do not involve an increase in payments when rates rise... recent research within the Federal Reserve suggests that many homeowners may have saved tens of thousands of dollars had they held adjustable-rate mortgages... to the degree that households are driven by fears of payment shocks but are willing to manage their own interest rate risks, the traditional fixed-rate mortgages may be an expensive way of financing a home."

ALAN GREENSPAN

Clever salespeople like Ralph used Greenspan's comments to encourage borrowers to take adjustable rate mortgages.

Why? Two reasons:

One, many borrowers could not qualify for the desired loan if the rate was fixed. In determining a borrower's ability to pay debt service, many underwriters – in a logic that defied explanation – used the ARM teaser rate even if it lasted for only a year or two.

Two, mortgage brokers often received higher fees for selling riskier (more expensive) loans. Last year the nation's largest mortgage lender, Countrywide, (now owned by Bank of America) was sued by several states. Among the allegations against Countrywide, the States claim that loan originators were encouraged to persuade borrowers to take out high-risk loans.

Greenspan's comments - suggesting that households should take adjustable rate loans and self-manage their interest rate risk (cut back on expenses and save for almost inevitable rate increases) – have been criticized in the financial press.

Some commentators have painted Greenspan as an intellectual out of touch with the average American household.

IVORY TOWER

145

"In any scrapbook of bad advice from economic gurus, that (Greenspan's suggestion about ARMS) should be near the top of the list."

CHARLES MORRIS

Charles Morris, author of *The Trillion Dollar Meltdown* (Perseus, 2008).

146

"Greenspan was extolling the virtues of floating – rate mortgages when interest rates were the lowest level they had been in over 50 years."

"Almost anyone who took that advice can not be happy with what has happened since he dispensed it."

"Once again the Chairman championed a cause that encouraged the public to behave in a way that most would come to regret."

WILLIAM FLECKENSTEIN

William Fleckenstein, author of *Greenspan's Bubbles: The of Age of Ignorance at the Federal Reserve* (McGraw-Hill, 2008)

148

149

"Oh, you'll see...
it's really quite
simple."

"OK! We're in!"

Ralph is a good salesman and he convinced Billy and Beth to pursue a Payment-Option ARM loan.

Some would argue that the short dialogue above between Ralph, and Billy and Beth, is an excellent window into what went wrong in the housing and lending worlds.

DID RALPH STEER BILLY AND BETH WRONG? YOU BE THE JUDGE.

1. <u>ADJUSTABLE RATE MORTGAGES (ARMS)</u>

Certainly in some situations the adjustable rate loan is a great product.

But were Billy and Beth advised of the risk?

Note that Ralph indicated that when the adjustable mortgage adjusts, the "loan rate can go up or down." This was disingenuous on Ralph's part because given very low initial rates (called "teasers"), the rate on adjustment would **most certainly go UP**.

In fact, many people following the housing world worry about teaser rates which reset (when the fixed period expires) in the next year or two. These analysts and commentators worry that when borrowers get their new mortgage invoices (with the reset rate), they will be shocked (and not in a nice way). That is why you may have heard people talk about the coming "rate shock."

Also, it was a little creepy of Ralph to quote Alan Greenspan in convincing Billy and Beth to pursue an adjustable loan. Ralph knew exactly what he was doing when he mentioned Greenspan's apparent support of ARMS … although Ralph himself had no clue what Greenspan was thinking.

2. PAYMENT-OPTION LOANS

Some experts would say that this loan product is the poster child for loan products that got people into trouble.

The logic of this loan (which also included very low teaser rates) was that the borrower had a choice: he or she could pay what was due or, he or she could pay less than what was due. If a borrower paid less than what was due, the difference was added onto the borrower's loan balance – what is called in the industry **negative amortization** (instead of a loan amortizing or getting smaller, it is getting larger and hence the term **negative** amortization).

Note, however, how clever Ralph was in describing the product. He emphasized its "flexibility." **And**, he never used the word "negative" amortization – because well, that term has such a NEGATIVE connotation. Instead he noted that the unpaid portion of the loan payment was **deferred**, meaning due at a later time. A mortgage broker friend of mine tells me that this choice of wording is very deliberate.

What is wrong with giving people the right to choose how much they want to pay every month?

Well, theoretically, nothing is wrong with that but some argue that in reality, by doing so, lenders gave borrowers too much leeway to get themselves into trouble.

With the whole world thinking that real estate prices were always going to go up, too many borrowers began to use their homes as an ATM machine.

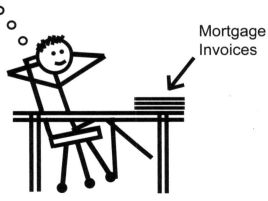

Let's see. I'm really tight this month and I would sure love to get a new car.

Mortgage Invoices

There was one other problem with Payment-Option ARM loans: prepayment penalties.

A prepayment penalty is a provision in a mortgage which deters a borrower from paying the loan off during the prepayment period.

So, even if a borrower wants to refinance (into a better and perhaps saner loan), he or she may not be able to.

Note that new regulations recently proposed by the Fed (with an effective date of October, 2009) will ban pre-payment penalties in certain situations.

There were two reasons for the prepayment penalty:

1. The lender had costs to originate the loan. In order to recoup its costs it needed the borrower to pay interest for some minimum period of time (the "pre-payment period").

2. The lender's largest cost was the mortgage broker (1% - 3% of the loan amount) – the lender had to earn enough interest to justify paying the mortgage broker's fee.

AS A RESULT, A MORTGAGE BROKER WHO WANTED TO EARN THE LARGEST FEE POSSIBLE NEEDED TO CONVINCE BORROWERS THAT TWO-TO-THREE-YEAR PREPAYMENT PERIODS WERE STANDARD CLAUSES IN ALL LOANS (THEY ARE NOT).

"Prepayment provisions are standard clauses in these loans."

BILLY

Ok let's recap:

1. Billy and Beth have decided to go for the Payment-Option ARM loan.

2. They have a rough understanding of what they are doing.

3. Ralph is afraid to explain any further – he feels he has them where he needs them.

4. **But, there is still one problem and it's a pretty big deal: Beth and Billy's credit score.**

Unfortunately for Billy and Beth their credit score is not very good.

You may have heard of FICO which is a formula for rating people's creditworthiness. FICO scores range from 300 to 850.

There are three large reporting agencies: TransUnion, Experian, and Equifax. Each company has its own system for collecting and reporting credit issues. Clever mortgage brokers learned how to manipulate the system and influence a client's credit score.

For example, in Mark Zandi's excellent book, *Financial Shock* (FT Press, 2008) he explains how some borrowers were able to instantly improve their credit score by becoming "authorized users" on credit card accounts of friends with better scores.

"Such transplanting of credit DNA wasn't wide-spread, but it shows how borrowers were able to game the system and affect lenders' models."

Author's Note:

My high school football coach would never use the word "problem." He said that word had a "negative" energy attached.

He said that there are "issues" or "situations" in life but never problems. My buddy broke his ankle and the bone was protruding. Coach said "looks like we have a situation here."

Today, whenever I hear someone use the word "situation," I immediately think "Oh crap, we have a real problem."

Ralph must think like my football coach.

"Unfortunately, your credit score is a bit lower than I had hoped... it's 550."

A credit score of 550 puts Billy and Beth into the sub-prime category.

Subprime means a loan that would not be purchased by the two largest buyers of U.S. mortgages – Fannie Mae and Freddie Mac.

As a result, Billy and Beth are going to pay an interest rate which is much higher than a borrower with a better credit score.

The word "subprime" was selected as the 2007 Word of the Year by the American Dialect Association – beating out "waterboarding."

174

175

"Well I've got some work to do but we should know in a few days."

IF YOU WERE A LENDER CONSIDERING BILLY AND BETH'S LOAN APPLICATION, WOULD YOU APPROVE IT?

1. They are putting down only 2% of the purchase price.

2. Their credit score indicates payment problems with creditors in the past twelve months.

3. Once their teaser rate adjusts, they are going to be stretched.

4. Although you are not supposed to know it (since Ralph forgot to tell you), Beth is leaving her job in the near future to go to law school.

BEFORE YOU ANSWER, LET'S PUT YOU INTO A LENDER'S CHAIR IN EARLY 2006:

1. Lenders were making lots of money originating and then selling loans to investment banks and investors.

2. In most situations, the lender had no obligation to the buyer of the loan if the borrower defaulted.

3. By 2006 competition to make loans had gotten very intense.

4. By 2006 most of the good credit borrowers with equity to invest had already purchased. Now almost every loan application you look at has one problem or another.

Here is how author Charles Morris, *The Trillion Dollar Meltdown* (Public Affairs, 2008) described the situation:

"By 2003 or so, mortgage lenders were running out of people they could plausibly lend to. Instead of curtailing lending they spread their nets to vacuum up prospects with little hope of repaying their loans. Subprime lending jumped from an annual volume of $145 billion in 2001 to $625 billion in 2005 … more than a third of subprime loans were for 100 percent of the home value …."

AND SO PERHAPS YOU WOULD HAVE APPROVED THE LOAN TO BILLY AND BETH...

In any event Ralph found a lender who did approve the loan.

Looks and sounds like a good loan to me.

BILLY AND BETH'S LENDER

As a result, Billy and Beth became one of thousands of borrowers in the subprime mortgage world.

Once again Billy and Beth have put themselves in a precarious position by not doing as much homework as they should have.

Perhaps an honorable mortgage broker could have found them a more conventional loan...or, given them arms-length advice about the entire process, causing them to reconsider their decision to buy at this time (high prices) and with 98% debt.

Some commentators believe that a major reason for the housing bust is that too many people put too much trust in their mortgage brokers.

Former Federal Reserve Governor, Ed Gramlich, had this to say about mortgage brokerage:

"One institution that has sprung up in the new mortgage market is that of the independent mortgage broker ... from an estimated 7,000 firms in 1987 to an estimated 53,000 firms in 2004 ... in 2005, about 60% of all sub-prime mortgages were place through brokers ... **brokers have minimal incentives to find the cheapest mort-gage for borrowers.**"

Subprime Mortgage: America's Latest Boom and Bust (Urban Institute, 2007)

Would Billy and Beth have been in a better situation if they went directly to a bank and worked with that bank's loan origination people?

Well, here is what Richard Bitner says about loan origination officers (many of whom were also compensated on a commission basis):

"When salespeople in any business are left to their own devices, they'll work the system to their benefit ... this is also true of the lender's account executives. With few rules and minimal consumer protections, abusive behavior flourished."

Billy and Beth's Closing

DISCLAIMER: THE AUTHOR IS A REAL ESTATE ATTORNEY. HE HATES LAWYER JOKES! WELL, EXCEPT THIS ONE:

Guy walks into a bar and orders a drink. Says to the bartender:

"All lawyers are greedy jerks."

"I'm outraged!"

"Ugh... a lawyer."

"Wrong, I'm a greedy jerk."

The reality of some closings is that in those cases when a borrower is represented by an attorney (in many states the closing is done by a title company), the attorney just wants the closing to occur as quickly as possible.

A borrower with a lot of questions or, who wants to review every document is sometimes seen as the enemy.

188

"I just have a dozen or so questions."

ATTORNEY

189

190

MANY BORROWERS ARE CONFUSED AND INTIMIDATED BY THE LOAN CLOSING.

You see, sometimes real estate attorneys and lenders are sued by litigator attorneys (the scourge of the earth) who claim that the real estate attorney or the lender did not make full disclosure to the borrower of the loan terms or, the risks involved.

As a result documents today contain **lots of disclosures.**

191

"Here's an important disclosure I'm supposed to read to you:

'The borrower acknowledges that it has been advised that the world could end at any time during the loan term, and that in the event it does, the borrower's obligation to the lender nevertheless continues and is not impacted thereby.'"

In part because of these disclosures and other self-protective language, the volume of paperwork at closing can be overwhelming. And, as a result, most borrowers – perhaps 90% – just stop reading, and sign, sign, sign.

(BILLY IS THERE SOMEWHERE)

Beth tires of asking questions. Her attorney has suggested that everything is standard form anyway. So, she and Billy sign, sign, sign.

"Have we finally signed everything?"

Lately, some academics claim that buyers and borrowers need more disclosures prior to or at closing.

Anyone thinking that disclosures are the answer is not familiar with the closing process. On or about closing few buyers have the time for or interest in disclosures, and the person responsible for reading or delivering them sometimes "pooh-pooh's" the message anyway.

What is needed is better education and financial literacy – disclosures at or about the time of closing are too little too late.

How many borrowers really understand what they are signing?

Well in a survey undertaken by the Federal Reserve in 2005 - 2006, titled "Do Homeowners Know Their House Values and Mortgage Terms?" it discovered that on average 1/3 of ARM borrowers did not understand several of the basic terms of their loans.

The fact is that the products were confusing, the documents were overwhelming, the attorneys or escrow officers entrusted with explaining the loans did not always do their jobs … and, as a result, borrowers were uninformed.

The key to averting problems in the future is NOT more disclosures. The key to averting problems in the future is to educate people before they even start the home buying or borrowing process.

WE NEED FINANCIAL LITERACY!!!!

Hey, and to the person reading this right now:

CONGRATULATIONS.

You are already 5 times more educated about the process than 90% of the people who bought homes and borrowed money in the last five years.

IN ANY EVENT, BILLY AND BETH'S CLOSING FINALLY
OCCURS. THE ATTORNEY IS HAPPY BECAUSE HE
MAKES HIS TEE TIME AND AN ELATED BILLY AND
BETH HEAD OFF TO THEIR NEW HOME.

UNFORTUNATELY,
THIS IS NOT
"THE END" OF
OUR STORY.

THE JOURNEY OF BILLY AND BETH'S LOAN

Billy and Beth's mortgage loan of $475,300 (98% of the $485,000 purchase price) now takes on a life of its own.

Let's follow the journey of this loan from its origination by the lender (National Lending) to its sale to an investment bank (World Investment Bank) and then to the subsequent securitization (defined below) and sale to an investor in Norway.

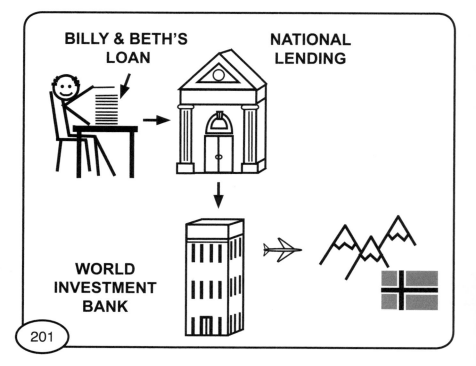

BILLY & BETH'S LOAN

NATIONAL LENDING

WORLD INVESTMENT BANK

Billy and Beth's lender, National Lending, was very good at originating high-yield (subprime) loans.

National knew that the loans it was making were high risk. But, because of that, National Lending could charge borrowers higher interest rates – in our example, three percentage points higher than a conventional loan.

NATIONAL LENDING COMPANY

"Nice job, guys. We've got $200 million in subprime product with an average interest rate of 8.5%. Time to call the investment banks."

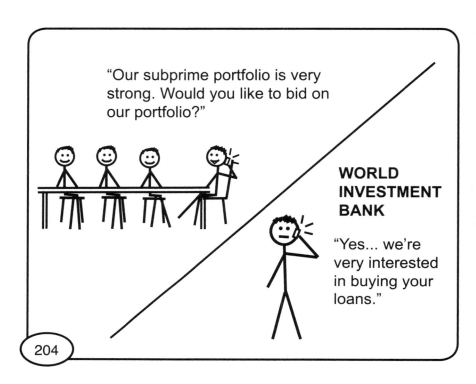

Now that World Investment Bank (Wall Street) is involved, the pace of our story picks up. Nowhere in the world are there more smart people creating ways to make money by moving paper around than on Wall Street.

For a well-written book on Wall Street's role in the housing crisis you might want to pick up:

Chain of Blame: How Wall Street Caused the Mortgage and Credit Crisis, Paul Muolo and Matthew Padilla (Wiley, 2008)

WHY DID THE INVESTMENT BANKS AND OTHER INVESTORS (E.G. HEDGE FUNDS) LOVE MORTGAGE LOANS?

1. The presumption in the investment community was that mortgages were safe investments. "People will always struggle to protect the investment in their homes" – was conventional thinking. But, this thinking was outdated in a lending mania when homebuyers had little money invested. When home values started to fall, some home-owners made rational decisions to default on mortgages that were higher in amount than the value of their homes.

2. The investment community also loved the yield of the higher risk mortgage loans – especially the subprime loans. As noted, these loans carried interest rates several points higher than conventional loans. And by leveraging the purchase of a subprime portfolio (i.e. borrowing to purchase the portfolio), the investment banks and others could really jack their return on investment.

Let's look at how the investment banker or hedge fund could pump the return on its purchase of a portfolio of subprime loans:

Say that World Investment Bank purchased the National Lending $200 million portfolio for $203 million (paying National a 1.5 point fee for the portfolio). Let's assume that World wanted to ramp up its return so it borrowed 90% of the $203 million that it paid to National. Let's assume that the interest rate on the money World borrowed was 5%.

Here is World's annual return on investment:

Interest received from National Portfolio

      8.5% x $200 million = $17,000,000

Interest paid on borrowed money
  90% x $203 million x 5% =   <u>$ 9,135,000</u>

             Cash Flow: $ 7,865,000

    World's capital (10%) = $20,300,000

RETURN = $7,865,000/$20,300,000 = 38.7%

This example is deliberately simplified.

Of course, when homeowners default the numbers sour pretty quickly.

For example, if 20% of the homeowners in the National Lending portfolio stop making interest payments, the return on World's investment drops dramatically:

Interest payments received = $13,600,000
Interest payments due on debt = $ 9,135,000
Net Cash Flow = $ 4,465,000

RETURN = $4,465,000/$20,300,000 = 21.9%

In other words, on a highly leveraged portfolio like this, a 20% drop in revenue causes almost a 50% drop in return on investment.

The fact that leverage is a double-edged sword is an important point people must understand – especially relevant when one purchases a home with lots of debt.

When one buys a home with a large mortgage, a relatively small drop in the value of the house can wipe out all of the homeowner's equity.

One question that a lot of people have asked me is how the very smart investment bankers could buy so many bad loans.

1. The investment bankers were on a tear to acquire loans – and just like home buyers caught in a mania, the investment bankers lost their head at times.

2. The investment bankers bought into the premise that U.S. housing prices never go down. Making that assumption, they did not properly analyze the risk of what they were doing.

3. Investment bankers – sitting on or around Wall Street – somehow missed what was happening on Main Street. They were removed from the down and dirty dealings going on between the buyer, the real estate agent, the mortgage broker, the lender – and other participants in the process.

4. Perhaps some investment bankers did know that they were in fact buying shaky loans – and that leads us to a big-deal topic:

SECURITIZATION

SECURITIZATION is the process by which the investment bankers would bundle many mortgage loans and use them as backing for financial instruments called MORTGAGE SECURITIES.

Think of a mortgage security as a bond, like a savings bond. When you purchase a U.S. savings bond, the government promises to pay you interest on your investment. Since you have the strength of the U.S. Treasury behind that commitment, you are certain to receive interest and, after some set period of time, your money back.

With a mortgage security, the investment banker makes no promises – just that the payments due under the mortgage security are backed by U.S. mortgages. As home-owners ("who never walk from their homes") pay their mortgages, the mortgage security pays its investors.

Until, of course, homeowners stop paying their mortgages.

CAUTION

**NEW WORD
COMING UP!**

TRANCHE
(French for "slice")

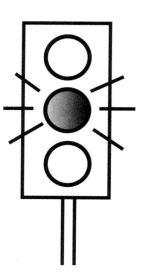

Investment banks knew that different investors had different risk tolerances.

So they created different levels of risk for investors interested in buying mortgage securities.

Those investors who were willing to take the highest risk got the highest return. These investors were in the lowest "tranche" of a mortgage security – payments to the investors in this tranche would be the first to stop if mortgages backing a particular security started to default (borrowers stopped paying).

Because investment bankers are so persuasive, the mortgage securitization business became very big.

Between 2002 and 2006 lenders and investment banks created a total of $2.3 trillion in mortgage securities.

The sale of mortgage securities to investors around the world became very profitable.

So investment bankers pulled out all stops to create a wide array of financial products backed by the "safety" of U.S. mortgage payments.

KEVIN PHILLIPS

"With profits and fees probably running up to $100 billion or more, inexcusable excesses were to be expected… the barons, princes and monarchs of finance turned to alchemists, this time mathematicians and options theorists, just as the fifteenth and sixteenth century princes and monarchs seeking gold and silver turned to metal-lurgical alchemists."

Bad Money (Viking, 2008)

"IF THIS IS ALL A BIT CONFUSING, DON'T WORRY. I AM A LITTLE CONFUSED MYSELF.

AND, IN FACT, SO ARE MANY OF THE INVESTORS WHO BOUGHT INTO INVESTMENT BANKER'S PITCHES ABOUT SAFE, PREDICTABLE, AND HIGH-YIELDING U.S. MORTGAGE SECURITIES!"

JIM RANDEL

Even the investment bankers selling the mortgage securities were confused.

The products created by the math geniuses were very convoluted. Sometimes the returns were bulked up by financing. Sometimes the returns from one security were dependent upon returns from another. The complexity could hurt sales.

The investment bankers knew that they needed some kind of "Good Housekeeping Seal of Approval."

ENTER THE RATINGS AGENCIES

There are three big ratings agencies in the United States: Fitch, Moody's and S&P.

These agencies have taken a lot of heat for their top AA and AAA ratings of certain mortgage securities and derivatives (investment vehicles created out of yield from other investment vehicles).

The concern was that the ratings agencies were too closely aligned with the investment banks issuing the mortgage securities the ratings agencies were evaluating.

The ratings agencies claimed that they maintained "Chinese Walls" (imaginary divisions) between their receipt of fees from the investment banks and, their ratings of securities issued by the investment banks.

INVESTMENT BANK

RATINGS AGENCY

CHINESE WALL

Some commentators are not so sure.

Richard Bitner: "Having the ratings agencies grade their investment-banker clients' securities is the equivalent of having a teacher write a student's term paper for him."

And Charles Morris has wondered out loud about how careful the ratings agencies could have been grading mortgage securities AA or AAA (tantamount to U.S. Treasuries) when shortly after the initial rating, the agencies downgraded some of these securities to junk status.

222

Postscript: A recent report by the Securities & Exchange Commission lambasted certain conduct of the ratings agencies.

Here are two e-mails the SEC quotes in its report, both sent by analysts at ratings agencies:

"Let's hope we are all wealthy and retired by the time this house of cards falters."

"It could be structured by cows and we would rate it."

The SEC report concludes that the ratings firms had run afoul of the basic guidelines intended to avoid conflicts of interest. DUH...

223

This whole process stinks a bit and one wonders whether it may hurt U.S. offerings in the future which seek to raise money from overseas investors:

"If the world loses confidence in the American markets, the long-term costs will be greater than a one-time trillion dollar balance sheet write down."

CHARLES MORRIS

But didn't the overseas investors understand what they were buying?

Here is an excerpt from *Chain of Blame*:

"If you ask (expert, Lew Ranieri) that question back in 2006, his answer would be an unequivocal 'no'.

'It's not what you disclosed; it's what you didn't'. He said investors didn't necessarily know what the borrower's combined loan-to-value ratio was, whether it was a real appraisal or one pulled off the Internet ... or, 'whether the guy (borrower) was a self-employed dish- washer'."

JANUARY, 2008

BILLY AND BETH ARE STARTING TO HAVE PROBLEMS.

The interest rate on their mortgage has reset and their monthly mortgage payment increased by $1,800.

What's more, Billy's new employer is worried about a softening economy. He did not give year-end bonuses.

Billy and Beth were counting on a year-end bonus to catch up on their bills. They cannot afford the $1,800 increase in their mortgage payment.

"Beth, I'm going to call Ralph and get the name of our banker. Someone I can explain our situation to."

Unfortunately for Billy and Beth, their lender had long since packaged their mortgage with others and sold it to World Investment Bank.

And, World Investment Bank used their mortgage (with many others) to create a mortgage security which was sold to investors in Europe.

In other words, there was no one entity or person who had enough of a stake in Billy and Beth's mortgage to want to speak with them.

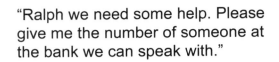

231

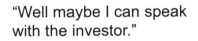

232

Although there were U.S. servicing companies (often owned by the original lender) handling the receipt of loan payments, these servicing companies:

1. Were understaffed and unable to deal with individual situations like Billy and Beth's.

2. Were overwhelmed when the housing crisis hit.

3. Had no incentive to create work-outs with individual borrowers.

In short, Ralph was correct: there was no one willing to speak with Billy and Beth about their problems.

Three months later, after having received 3 certified letters from an attorney stating an intention to foreclose and evict, Billy and Beth give up.

They spend all weekend lovingly cleaning up their home (not all borrowers do that) and on Monday mailed their keys (sometimes called "jingle mail") to the attorney's office.

Since their credit is damaged, they have trouble finding a nice rental and move back in with Beth's parents.

They are heartbroken.

By the way, Billy and Beth did explore refinancing. But, housing prices peaked in the 2nd quarter of 2006 and by the 1st quarter of 2008 their $485,000 house was worth only $425,000 such that refinancing was not an option.

BILLY AND BETH WERE VERY UNHAPPY LIVING WITH BETH'S PARENTS. A FEW WEEKS AFTER MOVING IN WITH THEM, THEY SEPARATED. BILLY MOVED OUT.

The investor who purchased the mortgage security backed in part by Billy and Beth's loan was not too happy either.

As Billy, Beth and many other U.S. homeowners began to default on their mortgages, the returns on the mortgage securities were not as promised.

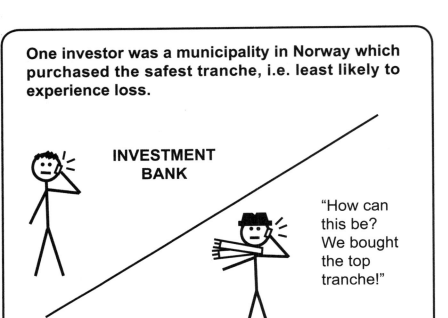

238

239

The conversation between disgruntled investors and investment bankers was probably a little more heated than what I have portrayed. But, what is the investment banker to say?

That the whole system was rigged?

By a government keeping interest rates artificially low... by real estate agents, appraisers and inspectors all with their hands out... by mortgage brokers and lenders with no skin in the game ... by investment bankers making huge fees creating securities that were far from secure... by conflicted ratings agencies.

The fact is that almost everyone in the progression from borrower to investor was assuming that U.S. home prices would always rise and therefore defaults would be rare.

The damage from this incorrect assumption was amplified by a lack of responsibility in the financial system.

"Of the places you can point the finger for the housing bubble … perhaps the most deserving is the removal of responsibility from the financial system. Lost in the rapid, wholesale rush to securitization … was the notion that someone – anyone – should ensure that individual loans are made responsibly, to responsible borrowers.

Securitization undermined this incentive for respon-sibility. No one had enough financial skin in the performance of any single loan to care whether it was good or not."

Mark Zandi, *Financial Shock* (FT Press, 2008)

As Zandi points out, everyone in the financial system – lenders, investment bankers, ratings agencies and investors - assumed that someone else was "minding the store," i.e., monitoring the process to be sure that loans were being carefully made to people who could pay them back. This presumption was faulty.

SPRING, 2009 ...

WHERE ARE WE TODAY?

Real estate prices have fallen dramatically since the beginning of 2006 when Billy and Beth purchased. According to the Case-Shiller/S&P report, the average median price of a U.S. home is down almost 30% since early 2006.

Why all of a sudden did housing prices start to fall in early '06?

There is no one reason.

Most would say that housing prices had been artificially propped up by low interest rates, easy money and buying mania. That it was inevitable prices would sooner or later return to earth.

Others blame the media who decided in 2006 that the big story was "The Boom has been Great, But is it time for the Bust?"

In fact, when I ask people in the real estate world what they think was the one factor that caused housing prices to tip, they all blame it on the media.

"If the media had not started writing that a bust was imminent, everything would have been fine. Buyers would have kept buying, prices would have kept rising, and lenders would have kept lending."

REAL ESTATE AGENT   **MORTGAGE BROKER**   **LENDER**   **REAL ESTATE ATTORNEY**

I GUESS THIS IS HOW MY FRIENDS IN THE REAL ESTATE WORLD SEE THE GENESIS OF THE PROBLEM:

"I'm bored."   "Me too."

JOURNALISTS

Blaming the crash on the media is a bit harsh. Whereas it is true that so long as people believe prices will go up, they tend to go up, there were fundamentals in play that caused prices to fall:

1. Too much debt caused increased defaults.

2. Investors of mortgage securities got nervous and funds for lending began to dry up.

3. Demand leveled – the numbers of people wanting or needing to buy decreased.

The fact is that we were in a buying mania and sooner or later, all the maniacs wake up!

EVENTUALLY ALL BOOMS COME TO AN END…

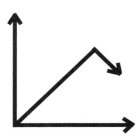

The problem with booms is the aggravating but inevitable busts that follow.

As economist John Kenneth Galbraith wrote in his book, *A Short History of Financial Euphoria* (Penguin, 1994), eventually there will be some event which spooks the boom and causes a rush for the exits.

And, unfortunately, usually the boom ends "not with a whimper, but with a bang."

This scenario describes today's housing and credit crisis.

Today's housing crisis was inevitable because sooner or later prices in every boom have to flatten or decline.

The problem with the housing boom was that prices **had to** keep rising in order to cover the many imprudent loans that lenders were making.

A house purchased for $X with too much debt did not present a problem so long as the house was worth $1.2X a year or so later. The owner could simply refinance, take out more debt, and pay any arrearage on the initial debt.

It was only when prices started to flatten and then fall that the real problems began, because only then was the entire system exposed for what it really was:

A HOUSE OF CARDS

AS OF THE SPRING OF 2009, IT IS ESTIMATED THAT 20% OR MORE OF ALL AMERICAN HOMEOWNERS WITH MORTGAGES ARE UNDER WATER.

IF PRICES CONTINUE TO DECLINE, THE HOUSING CRISIS COULD EXTEND WELL INTO 2010.

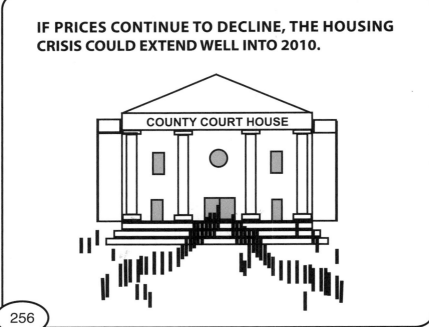

THE POINT OF OUR LITTLE BOOK IS TO IDENTIFY WHAT WE CAN LEARN FROM THIS EXPERIENCE… AND HOW WE CAN USE THAT INFORMATION TO MAKE OUR FINANCIAL LIVES BETTER …

1. Beware of buying mania... whenever someone tells you that the price of whatever is certain to go up, remind them of the 2009 Housing Crisis.

Throughout history there are always times when people lose their heads in a buying fervor.

Somehow we never seem to learn from history and from the words of those who have studied the psychology of mania. Here are some of my favorite quotes about speculative buying:

"(During times of speculation) normally sensible people drift into a behavior akin to that of Cinderella at the ball. They know that over-staying the festivities ... will eventually bring on pumpkins and mice. But they nevertheless hate to miss a single minute of what is one helluva party."

Warren Buffett

"Men and women proceeded to build a world of speculative make-believe. This is a world inhabited by people who ... want an excuse to believe. ... As time passes, the tendency to look beyond the simple fact of increasing values to the reason … greatly diminishes."

John Kenneth Galbraith *(speaking of the 1920's Florida real estate boom) The Great Crash 1929* (Houghton Mifflin,1954)

"A speculative bubble (is) a situation in which news of price increases spurs investor enthusiasm, which spreads by psychological contagion from person to person, in the process amplifying stories … despite doubts about the real value of the investment, (investors) are drawn to it partly through envy of others' successes and partly through gambler's excitement."

Robert Shiller
Irrational Exuberance (Doubleday, 2005)

AND, from a book written in 1841:

"Men, it has been said, think in herds; it will be seen that they go mad in herds, while they only recover their sense slowly, and one by one."

Charles Mackay
Extraordinary Popular Delusions (1841)

As you can see, it's not as if we weren't warned!!

2. Be wary of the kind of advice you receive from any business which is unregulated, easy to enter and requires little training.

"I hear we now need to take an exam."

"Count us out!"

ABC
MORTGAGE
BROKERS

---

3. Listen to financial advisors. They all advocate having three to six months of living expenses in a savings account. You never know when you might need that money, and decisions made in duress are usually not good ones!!

Remember Billy and Beth's experience when the bonus they counted on did not come through.

4. Buying a house is not brain surgery. Educate yourself about the market. Do not put all of your trust in anyone whose compensation model depends upon you to buy.

On the other hand, part of a successful house purchase is the formation of relationships with honest, hard-working professionals: a real estate agent, attorney, mortgage broker or lender, and house inspector.

In all of these categories, there are very ethical and knowledgeable individuals who can help you enormously. The key is to find people who will work for your best interest.

How do you find the right people?

Ask around. Friends and associates. People in Town Hall. <u>Anyone</u> who is <u>impartial</u>. Try to find someone who has just gone through the homebuying or selling experience.

5. When buying a house, understand the motivations and agenda of all the professionals you work with.

Real estate agents – work on commission

Mortgage brokers – work on commission

Loan origination officers – often work on commission

Home inspectors – some depend on agent referrals

Appraisers – some depend on mortgage broker referrals

The key is to be sure that those professionals "working for you" are **REALLY** working for you. If you understand how they make money, you can protect against a situation where their best interest is not your best interest.

You want them to make money. You just don't want them providing services or information inconsistent with your needs.

6. Lenders make money by inducing you to borrow. Then they want you to pay them lots of interest and perhaps some late fees and penalties. Do not expect your lender to respond warmly if you need a little forbearance on your debt repayments.

Gone are the days when there was a relationship between lender and borrower. Today, with securitization so prevalent (for all loans, not just mortgages) your "lender" may actually be an overseas investor who will not be interested in your personal problems.

Debt can actually be your best friend or, your worst enemy. Notwithstanding the advice of some writers to avoid debt if you can, the reality is that you probably can't. It is very hard to better your position unless you utilize debt – to your advantage. But first you need to understand lending practices … and, how to discipline yourself. We hope you will read how to build your self-discipline in our book:

The Skinny on Willpower

7. Do not depend upon the government to do your work for you. The goverment, too, has an agenda - not always in your best interest. Many people believe that had the Federal Reserve not kept interest rates artificially low during the housing boom (to meet the Administration's homeownership goals), we would not be in the mess we are in.

THE WHITE HOUSE

8. Wall Street is where a lot of really really smart people work and stay up late figuring out creative ways to separate others from their money.

Mortgage securities are just the latest bust – there will be others.

As former SEC Chairman Arthur Levitt has written in *Take on the Street: What Wall Street and Corporate America Don't Want You to Know* (Random House, 2002):

"I had spent twenty-eight years on Wall Street, and I understood the culture. Actually, there are two conflicting cultures. One rewarded professionalism, honesty and entrepreneurship. This recognized that without individual investors, the markets could not work. The other culture was driven by conflicts of interest, self-dealing and hype. It put Wall Street's short-term interests over investor interests. **This culture, regrettably, often overshadowed the other**." (Emphasis Added.)

9. There are often good reasons for waiting to buy a home.

Too many people have pressed the idea that buying a home is the best investment one can make. While there is certainly a lot to be said for paying down one's debt, instead of paying rent, there are also arguments to wait to buy.

1. Renting increases mobility. Real estate ownership is an illiquid investment and it is not always easy to get out of – renters today have much greater freedom than homeowners to move (i) to where the jobs are, and (ii) to the location most in sync with their lifestyle of choice.

2. Robert Kiyosaki in *Rich Dad, Poor Dad* (Tech Press, 1997) makes an excellent point. Homes consume money – they are therefore a liability. A young person might be well served to use his capital and earning power to invest in income-producing assets. There is always time to buy a home. Point: One should not necessarily buy a house just because he or she can.

10. Do not buy any product or make any investment that you do not fully understand. Each purchase or invest-ment decision you make can have a major impact on your future. You owe it to yourself to spend the time to become financially literate!

Most investments are within your ability to understand. And, if they are not … well, then pass on the "opportunity."

Ultimately, your only defense against the world's sharpies (and there are many of those) is your own SELF-EDUCATION and KNOWLEDGE. By becoming financially savvy, not only can you protect yourself against problems, but you can also position yourself to take the right steps to create wealth and financial independence.

In other words, do everything you can to become educated about money matters!

Now for some good news:

Billy and Beth reconciled!

The End

CONCLUSION

We hope that you have enjoyed our book.

For those of you who have a question, feel free to e-mail me at jrandel@theskinnyon.com.

I will endeavor to answer your question as quickly as I can.

With best regards,

Jim Randel

BIBLIOGRAPHY

We recommend the following twelve books as the best to read if you want to gain a more in-depth understanding of the housing and credit crisis:

Bad Money, Kevin Phillips (Viking, 2008)

Chain of Blame,
   Paul Muolo and Mathew Padilla (Wiley, 2008)

Confessions of a Subprime Lender,
   Richard Bitner (Wiley, 2008)

Extraordinary Popular Delusions,
   Charles Mackay (Harriman, 1841)

Financial Shock, Mark Zandi (FT Press, 2008)

Greenspan's Bubbles,
   William Fleckenstein (McGraw-Hill, 2008)

House Lust, Daniel McGinn (Doubleday, 2008)

Irrational Exuberance, Robert Shiller (Doubleday, 2005)

Sell Now, John Talbott (St. Martin's, 2006)

Subprime Mortgages,
   Edward Gramlich (Urban Institute, 2007)

The Great Crash 1929,
   John Kenneth Galbraith (Houghton Mifflin, 1954)

The Trillion Dollar Meltdown,
   Charles Morris (Public Affairs, 2008)

☡ the skinny on™ ☡
UPDATE

The Skinny on the Housing Crisis has just received first prize in the annual book competition sponsored by NAREE, the National Association of Real Estate Editors – an organization of 650 journalists and professionals who follow housing, finance, mortgages and business. This award was presented in Washington, D.C. on June 20th.

As for the housing crisis, we are finally seeing little glimmers of hope that the end may not be too far off. Prices are stabilizing in some markets, although at the lower end of the price spectrum. At least half of all purchases are distressed sales or first-time homebuyers buoyed by the $8,000 first-time buyer tax credit.

Unfortunately, foreclosures are continuing apace as more and more underwater borrowers are forced to, or choose to, walk from their homes. The Obama Administration's mortgage modification programs have not as yet taken hold and some experts predict 2 million foreclosures in 2009 and another 2 million in 2010. Foreclosures are, of course, a major problem because foreclosing lenders usually sell houses at depressed prices, which tends to drag down the whole market.

Right now the goal is for housing prices to stabilize. The next questions become whether and when we will see prices recover to the levels they were just a few years ago. No one knows for sure, of course, but most experts believe that it will be at least 5 years before we see prices rebound to 2005 – 2006 levels.

The upshot is that consumers need to become smarter buyers and borrowers. It is no longer enough to buy with the underlying assumption that prices will always rise and so what you pay and borrow are less important than just getting in the game. That assumption has proved to be faulty for millions of people. We at *The Skinny On* want you to be a savvier buyer/borrower – we hope that our book helps!!

AUTHOR BIO

Jim Randel, an attorney and graduate of Columbia Law School, has made his living as a real estate entrepreneur – buying and selling investment properties. For thirty years he has bought and sold single-family houses, small multi-family properties, apartment buildings, office buildings, retail centers, factories, warehouses and land.

Randel has also been a prolific writer and speaker on real estate-related topics. Prior to writing *The Skinny on the Housing Crisis*, he wrote *The Real Estate Game: And How to Win It* (CCH, 1986) and *Confessions of a Real Estate Entrepreneur* (McGraw-Hill, 2006).

Randel has been a guest speaker at many venues throughout the United States including Harvard and NYU Business Schools, the National Association of Realtors Annual Convention and numerous investor sessions.

Randel is considered a national authority on real estate topics. He has appeared on numerous radio and TV programs including CNBC, Fox and ABC. He is also a business columnist for The Huffington Post and is often quoted in major newspaper and internet outlets.

NOTES